50 Avocado Toast & Beyond Recipes

By: Kelly Johnson

Table of Contents

- Classic Avocado Toast with Sea Salt & Lemon
- Poached Egg Avocado Toast
- Smoked Salmon & Avocado Toast
- Avocado Toast with Cherry Tomatoes & Balsamic Glaze
- Spicy Sriracha Avocado Toast
- Everything Bagel Seasoned Avocado Toast
- Avocado Toast with Crispy Bacon & Chives
- Avocado & Hummus Toast
- Caprese Avocado Toast with Pesto
- Mediterranean Avocado Toast with Feta & Olives
- Avocado Toast with Radish & Microgreens
- Avocado & Goat Cheese Toast with Honey
- Avocado & Smoked Trout Toast
- Scrambled Eggs & Avocado Toast
- Avocado Toast with Roasted Sweet Potatoes
- Korean-Inspired Avocado Toast with Kimchi
- Buffalo Chicken Avocado Toast
- BLT Avocado Toast
- Avocado & Ricotta Toast with Hot Honey
- Avocado Toast with Fresh Strawberries & Balsamic
- Avocado & Black Bean Toast with Cotija Cheese
- Avocado Toast with Roasted Red Peppers & Arugula
- Avocado & Sardine Toast with Lemon Zest
- Spicy Chorizo & Avocado Toast
- Avocado Toast with Pickled Onions & Cilantro
- Tropical Avocado Toast with Mango & Coconut
- Avocado Toast with Soft-Boiled Egg & Chili Flakes
- Miso Avocado Toast with Sesame Seeds
- Avocado Toast with Pomegranate & Pistachios
- Mexican Street Corn Avocado Toast
- Avocado Toast with Crab Meat & Old Bay
- Roasted Mushroom & Avocado Toast
- Tahini Drizzled Avocado Toast
- Avocado Toast with Heirloom Tomatoes & Basil
- Greek Yogurt & Avocado Toast with Za'atar

- Avocado Toast with Roasted Chickpeas
- BBQ Jackfruit & Avocado Toast
- Beet & Avocado Toast with Feta
- Avocado Toast with Grilled Pineapple & Jalapeño
- Avocado & Cucumber Toast with Dill
- Avocado Toast with Seared Ahi Tuna
- Peanut Butter & Avocado Toast with Banana
- Avocado Toast with Smoked Gouda & Bacon Jam
- Avocado Toast with Roasted Garlic & Parmesan
- Vegan Avocado Toast with Tofu Scramble
- Pumpkin Seed & Avocado Toast
- Avocado Toast with Balsamic Caramelized Onions
- Grilled Peach & Avocado Toast
- Avocado Toast with Edamame & Furikake
- Avocado & Blue Cheese Toast with Walnuts

Classic Avocado Toast with Sea Salt & Lemon

Ingredients:

- 1 ripe avocado, mashed
- 2 slices sourdough or whole grain bread, toasted
- 1/2 tsp sea salt
- 1 tsp lemon juice

Instructions:

1. Mash avocado with lemon juice.
2. Spread on toasted bread and sprinkle with sea salt.

Poached Egg Avocado Toast

Ingredients:

- 1 ripe avocado, mashed
- 2 slices sourdough bread, toasted
- 2 eggs, poached
- Salt and black pepper, to taste

Instructions:

1. Spread mashed avocado on toast.
2. Top with poached eggs, season with salt and pepper.

Smoked Salmon & Avocado Toast

Ingredients:

- 1 ripe avocado, mashed
- 2 slices rye or whole grain bread, toasted
- 4 oz smoked salmon
- 1 tbsp cream cheese (optional)
- 1 tsp capers

Instructions:

1. Spread avocado (or cream cheese) on toast.
2. Top with smoked salmon and capers.

Avocado Toast with Cherry Tomatoes & Balsamic Glaze

Ingredients:

- 1 ripe avocado, mashed
- 2 slices sourdough bread, toasted
- 1/2 cup cherry tomatoes, halved
- 1 tbsp balsamic glaze

Instructions:

1. Spread avocado on toast.
2. Top with cherry tomatoes and drizzle with balsamic glaze.

Spicy Sriracha Avocado Toast

Ingredients:

- 1 ripe avocado, mashed
- 2 slices multigrain bread, toasted
- 1 tsp sriracha
- 1/2 tsp red pepper flakes

Instructions:

1. Spread avocado on toast.
2. Drizzle with sriracha and sprinkle red pepper flakes.

Everything Bagel Seasoned Avocado Toast

Ingredients:

- 1 ripe avocado, mashed
- 2 slices whole wheat bread, toasted
- 1 tbsp everything bagel seasoning

Instructions:

1. Spread avocado on toast.
2. Sprinkle everything bagel seasoning on top.

Avocado Toast with Crispy Bacon & Chives

Ingredients:

- 1 ripe avocado, mashed
- 2 slices sourdough bread, toasted
- 2 slices crispy bacon, crumbled
- 1 tbsp chives, chopped

Instructions:

1. Spread avocado on toast.
2. Top with crumbled bacon and chives.

Avocado & Hummus Toast

Ingredients:

- 1 ripe avocado, mashed
- 2 slices whole wheat bread, toasted
- 2 tbsp hummus
- 1/2 tsp paprika

Instructions:

1. Spread hummus on toast, then top with avocado.
2. Sprinkle with paprika before serving.

Caprese Avocado Toast with Pesto

Ingredients:

- 1 ripe avocado, mashed
- 2 slices sourdough bread, toasted
- 4 slices fresh mozzarella
- 4 cherry tomatoes, halved
- 1 tbsp pesto

Instructions:

1. Spread avocado on toast.
2. Top with mozzarella, tomatoes, and drizzle with pesto.

Mediterranean Avocado Toast with Feta & Olives

Ingredients:

- 1 ripe avocado, mashed
- 2 slices sourdough or whole wheat bread, toasted
- 1/4 cup crumbled feta cheese
- 2 tbsp chopped Kalamata olives
- 1 tsp olive oil
- 1/2 tsp dried oregano

Instructions:

1. Spread mashed avocado on toast.
2. Top with feta, olives, and a drizzle of olive oil.
3. Sprinkle with oregano before serving.

Avocado Toast with Radish & Microgreens

Ingredients:

- 1 ripe avocado, mashed
- 2 slices whole grain bread, toasted
- 2 radishes, thinly sliced
- 1/4 cup microgreens
- 1/2 tsp lemon juice
- Salt and pepper, to taste

Instructions:

1. Spread avocado on toast.
2. Top with sliced radish and microgreens.
3. Sprinkle with lemon juice, salt, and pepper.

Avocado & Goat Cheese Toast with Honey

Ingredients:

- 1 ripe avocado, mashed
- 2 slices sourdough bread, toasted
- 2 tbsp goat cheese, crumbled
- 1 tsp honey
- 1/4 tsp crushed red pepper flakes (optional)

Instructions:

1. Spread avocado on toast.
2. Top with crumbled goat cheese and drizzle with honey.
3. Sprinkle with red pepper flakes if desired.

Avocado & Smoked Trout Toast

Ingredients:

- 1 ripe avocado, mashed
- 2 slices rye or sourdough bread, toasted
- 4 oz smoked trout, flaked
- 1 tsp lemon zest
- 1/2 tsp fresh dill, chopped

Instructions:

1. Spread avocado on toast.
2. Top with smoked trout and sprinkle with lemon zest and dill.

Scrambled Eggs & Avocado Toast

Ingredients:

- 1 ripe avocado, mashed
- 2 slices multigrain bread, toasted
- 2 eggs, scrambled
- 1 tbsp butter
- Salt and pepper, to taste

Instructions:

1. Spread avocado on toast.
2. Scramble eggs in butter and place on top.
3. Season with salt and pepper.

Avocado Toast with Roasted Sweet Potatoes

Ingredients:

- 1 ripe avocado, mashed
- 2 slices whole wheat bread, toasted
- 1/2 cup roasted sweet potatoes, cubed
- 1 tsp olive oil
- 1/2 tsp smoked paprika

Instructions:

1. Roast sweet potatoes at **400°F (200°C) for 20 minutes**.
2. Spread avocado on toast and top with sweet potatoes.
3. Drizzle with olive oil and sprinkle with smoked paprika.

Korean-Inspired Avocado Toast with Kimchi

Ingredients:

- 1 ripe avocado, mashed
- 2 slices sourdough bread, toasted
- 1/4 cup kimchi, chopped
- 1 tsp sesame seeds
- 1/2 tsp gochujang (Korean chili paste)

Instructions:

1. Spread avocado on toast.
2. Top with kimchi and drizzle with gochujang.
3. Sprinkle with sesame seeds.

Buffalo Chicken Avocado Toast

Ingredients:

- 1 ripe avocado, mashed
- 2 slices whole grain bread, toasted
- 1/2 cup shredded chicken
- 2 tbsp buffalo sauce
- 1 tbsp blue cheese crumbles

Instructions:

1. Toss shredded chicken with buffalo sauce.
2. Spread avocado on toast and top with buffalo chicken.
3. Sprinkle with blue cheese crumbles.

BLT Avocado Toast

Ingredients:

- 1 ripe avocado, mashed
- 2 slices sourdough bread, toasted
- 4 slices crispy bacon
- 4 cherry tomatoes, halved
- 1 lettuce leaf, chopped

Instructions:

1. Spread avocado on toast.
2. Top with bacon, tomatoes, and lettuce.

Avocado & Ricotta Toast with Hot Honey

Ingredients:

- 1 ripe avocado, mashed
- 2 slices whole wheat bread, toasted
- 1/4 cup ricotta cheese
- 1 tsp hot honey

Instructions:

1. Spread ricotta on toast, then top with avocado.
2. Drizzle with hot honey before serving.

Avocado Toast with Fresh Strawberries & Balsamic

Ingredients:

- 1 ripe avocado, mashed
- 2 slices sourdough bread, toasted
- 4 fresh strawberries, sliced
- 1 tsp balsamic glaze
- 1/2 tsp honey (optional)

Instructions:

1. Spread mashed avocado on toast.
2. Top with strawberries and drizzle with balsamic glaze.
3. Add honey for extra sweetness if desired.

Avocado & Black Bean Toast with Cotija Cheese

Ingredients:

- 1 ripe avocado, mashed
- 2 slices whole wheat bread, toasted
- 1/4 cup black beans, mashed or whole
- 2 tbsp Cotija cheese, crumbled
- 1/2 tsp lime juice
- 1/4 tsp cumin

Instructions:

1. Spread mashed avocado on toast.
2. Top with black beans and Cotija cheese.
3. Sprinkle with cumin and lime juice before serving.

Avocado Toast with Roasted Red Peppers & Arugula

Ingredients:

- 1 ripe avocado, mashed
- 2 slices sourdough bread, toasted
- 1/4 cup roasted red peppers, sliced
- 1/4 cup fresh arugula
- 1 tsp olive oil
- Salt and black pepper, to taste

Instructions:

1. Spread avocado on toast.
2. Top with roasted red peppers and arugula.
3. Drizzle with olive oil and season with salt and pepper.

Avocado & Sardine Toast with Lemon Zest

Ingredients:

- 1 ripe avocado, mashed
- 2 slices rye bread, toasted
- 1 small can sardines, drained
- 1 tsp lemon zest
- 1/2 tsp fresh parsley, chopped

Instructions:

1. Spread avocado on toast.
2. Place sardines on top and sprinkle with lemon zest and parsley.

Spicy Chorizo & Avocado Toast

Ingredients:

- 1 ripe avocado, mashed
- 2 slices sourdough bread, toasted
- 1/4 cup cooked chorizo, crumbled
- 1/2 tsp red pepper flakes

Instructions:

1. Spread avocado on toast.
2. Top with chorizo and sprinkle with red pepper flakes.

Avocado Toast with Pickled Onions & Cilantro

Ingredients:

- 1 ripe avocado, mashed
- 2 slices whole grain bread, toasted
- 1/4 cup pickled red onions
- 1 tbsp fresh cilantro, chopped

Instructions:

1. Spread avocado on toast.
2. Top with pickled onions and cilantro.

Tropical Avocado Toast with Mango & Coconut

Ingredients:

- 1 ripe avocado, mashed
- 2 slices multigrain bread, toasted
- 1/4 cup fresh mango, diced
- 1 tbsp shredded coconut
- 1/2 tsp lime juice

Instructions:

1. Spread avocado on toast.
2. Top with mango and shredded coconut.
3. Drizzle with lime juice.

Avocado Toast with Soft-Boiled Egg & Chili Flakes

Ingredients:

- 1 ripe avocado, mashed
- 2 slices sourdough bread, toasted
- 2 soft-boiled eggs, halved
- 1/2 tsp red chili flakes

Instructions:

1. Spread avocado on toast.
2. Top with soft-boiled eggs and sprinkle with chili flakes.

Miso Avocado Toast with Sesame Seeds

Ingredients:

- 1 ripe avocado, mashed
- 2 slices whole grain bread, toasted
- 1/2 tsp white miso paste
- 1 tsp sesame seeds (black or white)

Instructions:

1. Mix miso paste into mashed avocado.
2. Spread on toast and sprinkle with sesame seeds.

Avocado Toast with Pomegranate & Pistachios

Ingredients:

- 1 ripe avocado, mashed
- 2 slices whole wheat bread, toasted
- 2 tbsp pomegranate seeds
- 1 tbsp pistachios, chopped

Instructions:

1. Spread avocado on toast.
2. Top with pomegranate seeds and chopped pistachios.

Mexican Street Corn Avocado Toast

Ingredients:

- 1 ripe avocado, mashed
- 2 slices sourdough bread, toasted
- 1/2 cup grilled corn
- 2 tbsp Cotija cheese, crumbled
- 1/2 tsp chili powder
- 1 tsp lime juice
- 1 tbsp fresh cilantro, chopped

Instructions:

1. Spread mashed avocado on toast.
2. Top with grilled corn, Cotija cheese, and chili powder.
3. Drizzle with lime juice and sprinkle with cilantro.

Avocado Toast with Crab Meat & Old Bay

Ingredients:

- 1 ripe avocado, mashed
- 2 slices sourdough or rye bread, toasted
- 1/2 cup fresh crab meat
- 1/2 tsp Old Bay seasoning
- 1 tsp lemon juice
- 1 tbsp chives, chopped

Instructions:

1. Spread avocado on toast.
2. Top with crab meat, Old Bay seasoning, and lemon juice.
3. Garnish with chopped chives.

Roasted Mushroom & Avocado Toast

Ingredients:

- 1 ripe avocado, mashed
- 2 slices whole grain bread, toasted
- 1/2 cup roasted mushrooms (shiitake, cremini, or portobello)
- 1/2 tsp garlic powder
- 1 tbsp balsamic glaze

Instructions:

1. Roast mushrooms with garlic powder at **400°F (200°C) for 15 minutes**.
2. Spread avocado on toast and top with roasted mushrooms.
3. Drizzle with balsamic glaze before serving.

Tahini Drizzled Avocado Toast

Ingredients:

- 1 ripe avocado, mashed
- 2 slices multigrain bread, toasted
- 1 tbsp tahini
- 1/2 tsp lemon juice
- 1/2 tsp sesame seeds

Instructions:

1. Spread avocado on toast.
2. Drizzle with tahini and lemon juice.
3. Sprinkle with sesame seeds.

Avocado Toast with Heirloom Tomatoes & Basil

Ingredients:

- 1 ripe avocado, mashed
- 2 slices sourdough bread, toasted
- 1/2 cup heirloom cherry tomatoes, sliced
- 1 tbsp fresh basil, chopped
- 1 tsp balsamic glaze

Instructions:

1. Spread avocado on toast.
2. Top with heirloom tomatoes and basil.
3. Drizzle with balsamic glaze.

Greek Yogurt & Avocado Toast with Za'atar

Ingredients:

- 1 ripe avocado, mashed
- 2 slices whole wheat bread, toasted
- 2 tbsp Greek yogurt
- 1/2 tsp za'atar seasoning
- 1/2 tsp olive oil

Instructions:

1. Spread Greek yogurt on toast, then top with avocado.
2. Sprinkle with za'atar and drizzle with olive oil.

Avocado Toast with Roasted Chickpeas

Ingredients:

- 1 ripe avocado, mashed
- 2 slices whole grain bread, toasted
- 1/2 cup roasted chickpeas
- 1/2 tsp smoked paprika
- 1 tsp lemon juice

Instructions:

1. Roast chickpeas at **400°F (200°C) for 20 minutes** with smoked paprika.
2. Spread avocado on toast and top with roasted chickpeas.
3. Drizzle with lemon juice before serving.

BBQ Jackfruit & Avocado Toast *(Vegan)*

Ingredients:

- 1 ripe avocado, mashed
- 2 slices whole grain bread, toasted
- 1/2 cup shredded jackfruit
- 2 tbsp BBQ sauce
- 1 tbsp red onion, chopped

Instructions:

1. Sauté jackfruit in BBQ sauce for **5 minutes**.
2. Spread avocado on toast and top with BBQ jackfruit.
3. Garnish with chopped red onion.

Beet & Avocado Toast with Feta

Ingredients:

- 1 ripe avocado, mashed
- 2 slices rye or sourdough bread, toasted
- 1/2 cup roasted beets, diced
- 2 tbsp feta cheese, crumbled
- 1 tsp balsamic glaze

Instructions:

1. Spread avocado on toast.
2. Top with roasted beets and feta.
3. Drizzle with balsamic glaze before serving.

Avocado Toast with Grilled Pineapple & Jalapeño

Ingredients:

- 1 ripe avocado, mashed
- 2 slices whole grain bread, toasted
- 2 slices grilled pineapple
- 1/2 jalapeño, thinly sliced
- 1/2 tsp lime juice
- 1/4 tsp chili flakes

Instructions:

1. Grill pineapple slices until caramelized.
2. Spread avocado on toast and top with pineapple and jalapeño.
3. Drizzle with lime juice and sprinkle chili flakes.

Avocado & Cucumber Toast with Dill

Ingredients:

- 1 ripe avocado, mashed
- 2 slices rye or whole wheat bread, toasted
- 1/2 cucumber, thinly sliced
- 1 tbsp fresh dill, chopped
- 1/2 tsp lemon juice
- Salt and black pepper, to taste

Instructions:

1. Spread avocado on toast.
2. Top with cucumber slices and sprinkle with dill.
3. Drizzle with lemon juice and season with salt and pepper.

Avocado Toast with Seared Ahi Tuna

Ingredients:

- 1 ripe avocado, mashed
- 2 slices sourdough bread, toasted
- 4 oz ahi tuna, seared and sliced
- 1/2 tsp sesame seeds
- 1/2 tsp soy sauce
- 1/2 tsp wasabi mayo (optional)

Instructions:

1. Sear ahi tuna for **1 minute per side**, then slice thinly.
2. Spread avocado on toast and top with tuna.
3. Drizzle with soy sauce and sprinkle sesame seeds.

Peanut Butter & Avocado Toast with Banana

Ingredients:

- 1 ripe avocado, mashed
- 2 slices whole wheat bread, toasted
- 2 tbsp peanut butter
- 1/2 banana, sliced
- 1 tsp honey

Instructions:

1. Spread peanut butter on toast, then add mashed avocado.
2. Top with banana slices and drizzle with honey.

Avocado Toast with Smoked Gouda & Bacon Jam

Ingredients:

- 1 ripe avocado, mashed
- 2 slices sourdough bread, toasted
- 2 slices smoked Gouda cheese
- 2 tbsp bacon jam

Instructions:

1. Spread avocado on toast.
2. Top with smoked Gouda and bacon jam.

Avocado Toast with Roasted Garlic & Parmesan

Ingredients:

- 1 ripe avocado, mashed
- 2 slices multigrain bread, toasted
- 1/2 head roasted garlic, mashed
- 2 tbsp grated Parmesan
- 1 tsp olive oil

Instructions:

1. Mix roasted garlic into mashed avocado.
2. Spread on toast and top with Parmesan.
3. Drizzle with olive oil.

Vegan Avocado Toast with Tofu Scramble

Ingredients:

- 1 ripe avocado, mashed
- 2 slices whole grain bread, toasted
- 1/2 cup crumbled tofu
- 1/2 tsp turmeric
- 1/2 tsp nutritional yeast
- 1 tbsp olive oil

Instructions:

1. Sauté tofu with turmeric, nutritional yeast, and olive oil for **5 minutes**.
2. Spread avocado on toast and top with tofu scramble.

Pumpkin Seed & Avocado Toast

Ingredients:

- 1 ripe avocado, mashed
- 2 slices whole grain bread, toasted
- 2 tbsp toasted pumpkin seeds
- 1/2 tsp sea salt
- 1/2 tsp lime juice
- 1/4 tsp smoked paprika

Instructions:

1. Spread avocado on toast.
2. Top with toasted pumpkin seeds.
3. Sprinkle with sea salt, smoked paprika, and drizzle with lime juice.

Avocado Toast with Balsamic Caramelized Onions

Ingredients:

- 1 ripe avocado, mashed
- 2 slices sourdough bread, toasted
- 1/2 cup caramelized onions
- 1 tbsp balsamic glaze
- 1/2 tsp thyme (optional)

Instructions:

1. Caramelize onions by cooking them on low heat for **20 minutes** with a splash of balsamic glaze.
2. Spread avocado on toast and top with caramelized onions.
3. Drizzle with additional balsamic glaze and sprinkle with thyme.

Grilled Peach & Avocado Toast

Ingredients:

- 1 ripe avocado, mashed
- 2 slices sourdough or whole grain bread, toasted
- 1 peach, sliced and grilled
- 1 tsp honey
- 1 tbsp crumbled feta cheese
- 1/2 tsp black pepper

Instructions:

1. Grill peach slices for **2-3 minutes per side**.
2. Spread avocado on toast and top with grilled peaches.
3. Drizzle with honey, sprinkle with feta and black pepper.

Avocado Toast with Edamame & Furikake

Ingredients:

- 1 ripe avocado, mashed
- 2 slices multigrain bread, toasted
- 1/4 cup shelled edamame
- 1 tsp furikake seasoning
- 1/2 tsp sesame oil

Instructions:

1. Spread avocado on toast.
2. Top with edamame and sprinkle with furikake.
3. Drizzle with sesame oil before serving.

Avocado & Blue Cheese Toast with Walnuts

Ingredients:

- 1 ripe avocado, mashed
- 2 slices whole wheat bread, toasted
- 2 tbsp crumbled blue cheese
- 2 tbsp chopped walnuts
- 1/2 tsp honey

Instructions:

1. Spread avocado on toast.
2. Top with blue cheese and walnuts.
3. Drizzle with honey before serving.

www.ingramcontent.com/pod-product-compliance
Lightning Source LLC
LaVergne TN
LVHW061953070526
838199LV00060B/4091